ASTROLOGY—

What Your Stars Foretell

ASTROLOGY —
WHAT YOUR STARS FORETELL

By

MARIE-SIMONE

Marie-Simone has donated her fee for the writing of this book to the Leukaemia Research Fund, Institute of Child Health, Great Ormond Street, London, W.C.1.

MAGNA PRINT BOOKS
LITTON, YORKSHIRE.

First Published in large print 1975
by
Magna Print Books,
Litton, Skipton, Yorkshire.
by arrangement with
W. & G. Foyle Limited
London

ISBN 0 86009 033 7

Printed in Great Britain

CONTENTS

ZODIACAL CHARACTER ANALYSES

INTRODUCTION

ASTROLOGY is the oldest of the occult sciences and is enjoying in this modern age a following larger than ever before in its long history. The famous and the infamous, the rich and the poor, the arrogant and the humble, the powerful and those without power, philosophers and others of great wisdom and learning have found...and are finding...need to recourse to it. All and sundry have indeed frequently profited from either direct application or by heeding the advice offered by those best qualified to interpret the astral portents for them. In the high-pressured existence of the 20th Century ever more and more men and women from all walks of life are seeking...and finding...solace, hope, renewed faith in life's purpose. Only by accepting Man's oneness with the cosmos, by accepting the unity of all life in the Universe can purpose to existence be conceived and comprehended.

The logic of this is incredibly lacking in complexity. Not even the "Flat-earthers" seriously dispute that the Sun and Moon have strong influence on Earthly Life. Both play significant and very effective parts in the lives of individuals, families and nations. Poets, romantics, sailors and others have never doubted the influence not only of Sun and Moon but also of Planets and Stars. Therefore to deny such influence dogmatically would seem neither logical nor scientific. It is now almost universally accepted that, *"as above, so below"*. The microcosm reflects the macrocosm as surely as the sea reflects the sky above it. We now know...revealed by modern science, predicted by Astrology...that the atom is a tiny solar system. It therefore follows that Man, composed of atoms...made up of millions and millions of small solar systems...must indeed be part of *the* solar system and thus part of the cosmic whole.

But it has taken many, many centuries of empirical observations, much trial and error, much shedding of superstition for Astrology to approach the orderly and reputable society that is modern Western Astrology. My own Astrological system could be said to have descended almost directly from one of the greatest Astrologers in history...Claudius Ptolemy. A great Astrologer, astronomer and mathematician. Just as his work *Almagest* handed down to us the

Ptolemaic system of the Universe so it must be said his astonishingly erudite book on Astrology *Tetrabiblios...Four Books on the Influence of the Stars*...remained the leading authoritative text for nearly sixteen centuries. His science was more sophisticated than that of the Middle Ages so long after him. He taught that Man, by predicting the future as revealed by the Stars, by being forewarned and forearmed, could be prepared to take advantage of opportunities arising whilst being alert against possible adversity. He showed that the Reading of the Stars could prepare Man for all exigencies...favourable or otherwise. Whereas medieval Astrology degraded the science, tainted it with superstition by demanding propitiation of "bad-luck stars" and ritualistic thanksgiving to "good-luck stars" to a Pagan degree. Thus falling into disrepute and...justifiably...incurring the disapproval of the Church.

The origins of Astrology are indeed remote. The King of Assyria during the years 669 to 626 B.C. mentions works said to have been written on Astrology in the days of the Sumerian King Sargon of Agade as early as 3000 B.C. From these ancient times...and from earlier, prehistoric ages...through the Babylonians and Assyrians (now referred to as Chaldeans) and via the Hebrews, Greeks, Chinese, Arabs, Romans and Christians the modern science has developed. The earliest record we have depicting the Houses of the Horoscope more or less as we know them today dates from the 13th century...the system attributed to one, Campanus, chaplain, physician and mathematician to Pope Urban IV.

An exceedingly renowned Astronomer, Nostradamus, born at St. Remy in 1503 and who was Astronomer Royal to three French kings predicted such long-range events as the rise of Cromwell, that of Napoleon and the date of the Second World War. His quatrains, too obscure for his contemporaries, are still consulted, and the key to his chronology sought.

The Danes produced a most important astronomer-astrologer in Tycho Brahe (1546-1601) who was patronised by King Frederick II. He corrected and improved the astronomical tables of the famous Copernicus.

The most renowned of the English Astrologers was William Lilly who, born in 1602, cast a Horoscope for King Charles I *two whole years before his execution* part of which he interpreted as follows: "Luna is with Antares, a violent fixed Star which is said to denote violent death, and Mars, which is approaching Caput Algol, which is said to denote *beheading,* might intimate that." Among other things he also predicted accurately the Great Fire of London.

Modern Astrology...especially Western...has been able quite successfully to discard the superstitious encumbrances of the early Middle Ages... while retaining the traditional language...and is able, from cumulative experience and knowledge accruing over thousands of years coupled with the use of up-to-date technology...predicted by Astrologers...to apply the ancient wisdom, the Ptolemaic sophistication with scientific revelation, to give yet greater service to Mankind.

Astrology is a science of Movement. By its very nature as a subject it cannot be static. Movement, movement, on, ever on. Progress. Mobility. Development. Motion is the Key! The planets and the Stars inexorably move on, on through the heavens, through the Zodiac. As all life moves. To stop and live is impossible. We are, each and every single one of us, caught up in this vast Cosmic Stream. By accepting the obvious, by not drifting like dead logs at the mercy of wind and current, we can ride the storms, negotiate the rapids, glide more smoothly along the wider, less turbulent reaches. If there

is doubt as to our being absolute Masters of ou
Destiny we can ensure that we are not its Slaves
Simply by heeding the wondrous message writter
in our Stars.

To accept Astrology at all we must accept i
seriously. A Personal Horoscope can be equated
with a psychological analysis...of which it wa
the father. To attempt to journey through Lif
without a Horoscope is about as hazardous and
as foolhardy as to try travelling through dens
jungle minus a compass. All Cosmos, includin
Man, is subject to the same universal Laws. Bu
Man has been given the Power of Thought, *i*
being aware of the Laws, apply such Thought
Reasoning and Knowledge advantageously.

There is an astonishingly simple lesson to b
learned from the Stars. It is the lesson of Livin
for Today. The Stars *demand* nothing. It is th
interpretation of the Reading of them, th
understanding of the Aspects, the various con
junctions which can forewarn and thus arm. S
that, correctly used, Astrology can teach us t
live only for this day...with, of course, certai
reservations as indicated in our Personal Horos
copes. It can teach us not to struggle futilely
not to attempt to solve all Life's seemingl
insoluble problems in any one day. An intelligen

appraisal of the Astral indications can inform just what action...or quite as important *inaction* ...can be taken today, whether the action actually concerns today or some future date. What we now begin to appreciate is that the Stars reveal to us exactly how to make the very best of ourselves, how to discover our most exalted form of self-expression. In short...*how to fulful*!

Astrology, ever triumphant, has not re-emerged so victoriously from the superstition of the Dark Ages to *challenge*. Great thinkers through the years, and those of today, have known, and know, that Astrology *shares,* and does not query, the marvellous grandeur of Philosophy and all the important religions. Jung himself never ceased to expound the many parallels between Astrology and Psychology. The ancient concepts are now reinforced with up-to-the-minute technology. The Cosmic Stream, the Whole of which we are each a vital part, is not merely the starting place for observation...it is the Subject. It is Us and Life and the Laws. As we are It.

Few things are hidden from the reputable Astrologer. Given the refined research methods available today fewer things need be hidden.

THE PLANETS

ORIGINALLY five planets were known to the Babylonians. Through the successive ages these Planets were named and renamed by the Egyptians, Greeks, Romans. Modern Astrology continues to use the Roman names.

Uranus, a new Planet, was discovered in 1781 by Sir William Herschel. A further Planet in 1846 named Neptune was discovered and Pluto in 1930. Taking 284 years, as it does, to travel through the Zodiac this Planet exerts but rather slight influence on Personal Horoscopes.

The Planets are like keynotes to the Signs. Most modern Astrologers for the sake of convenience consider Sun and Moon to be "planets". Finding this usage astrologically and astronomically incorrect however I prefer to call them simply "Rulers" and the remainder "Ruling Planets". It will be seen, therefore, that there are five Ruling Planets and two Rulers...Sun and Moon.

Sun, centre of our solar system, is the mos

important Ruler in the Horoscope. Source of Life, he links us irrevocably to the Sign in which he is situated at the time of our birth. He gives us Individuality and, further, this position at birth gives us our basic temperament while Moon and the Planets will give means of expression.

These two Rulers, Sun and Moon, more than any of the Planets take on their hue from the Sign in which they are placed...though this is qualified by the positioning...the "aspects"...at the time—and the Sign. (It is beyond the scope of this book to go deeply into the technical complexities of the practical Science of Astrology but, in passing, it must be explained that an "aspect" is known by calculating the angular separation of one Planet from another or from the Sun or Moon. These distances are measured in degrees, minutes and seconds. A simple example is the trine. If a Planet is 120° away from another they are in an aspect of "trine". This is a favourable Aspect...viz of co-operation and construction.) Loosely it can be said that these two Rulers take on in the Horoscope not only the characteristics of the Sign of the Zodiac but the nature of the Birthdate.

Further to being the Individuality, Sun in the Personal Horoscope presents Will...the Urge of

Ego. The Sun is symbolic of Power and Authority. But the Power is based on admiration and affection rather than Force.

Moon, the "External Being", contrasts to Sun in being sentimental, sympathetic, changeable and maternal. She translates the vitality of Sun into action insofar as her position in the Horoscope and Sun's strength permit. She is the basis of the map so to speak. Being the Sign of the Home...which is the foundation upon which our lives are built. How we express ourselves to the world depends largely upon early environment and family background, and this is the part Moon plays in our Horoscopes.

She is The Great Mother. And can be loving and compassionate or possessive and quite selfish. She represents magnetic Personality, sensitiveness and can be unreliable, evasive, bewildering.

It can be seen, then, that these two Rulers, Sun and Moon, make...with the Sign of the Zodiac itself...the initial keys to character analysis. Sun is the first. It shows the subject's basic character but is mainly concerned with spiritual qualities. The Zodiacal Sign rising at the time of birth is the second key and influences the physical body and enhances or weakens the tendencies of the Sun. The third vital key will be found in the position of Moon at birth. She primarily affects the subconscious. As this in turn affects the conscious. All thought, action and Personality are therefore influenced.

The Ruling Planet Mercury, "Messenger of the Gods", reveals the workings of the mind and communication of ideas. He can be influenced for good or evil. Depending on his proximity to either Jupiter or Saturn. Although Mercury is generally referred to masculinely it is considered hermaphrodite. On the mental rather than physical plane...therefore neutral, impersonal. Restless, nervous, changeable, his inquisitiveness is boundless and he is a fast talker and a quick thinker. Mercury is Mutable. And mutation...or change...is the essence of his being. He is naturally clever and astute, and most things come easily to him...intellectually or otherwise. For, astonishingly, he is also adept with his hands. A person with a strong Mercury can be a very paradoxical person indeed. Cleverer, more ingenious than most at getting himself out of sticky situations without too keen a regard for truth, he nevertheless has an intense fondness for facts. One given to explaining the ideas and creations of others rather than creating himself.

Usually he possesses an enormous fund of miscellaneous information and knowledge which, at a moment's notice, he can turn to advantage.

In short, Mercury has a subtle brain and intellect, is dignified, can dispute with learned discretion and eloquence. He can produce wonders.

Venus has retained most of the characteristics of her Babylonian original, is, like Moon, feminine. In her positive manifestations she influences the ability to fascinate, to attract, to love and to express art. She is of the sea, born from its foam, and rules Love, nature, children, pleasure, luck, wealth and art. She makes singers as well as fanatical lovers of flowers. She represents elegance, gentility, benevolence, tenderness.

On the negative side Venus produces weaklings leaning towards erotic and frivolous pasttimes, can display ostentatious bad taste or be in many other ways emotionally immature.

Summing up, Venus is at her best when in Taurus...goddess of the Earth. Or as the Earthly bride in Libra, the mystical bride in Pisces. In Scorpio we find her as the intense, seductive lover. And in Virgo, the critical virgin.

Mars is the fiery Planet. The Planet of energy

and initiative...of beginnings and endings. "Fiery, violent...a destroyer...delighting in slaughter and death, in quarrels, brawls, dispute...is quickly moved to vehemence and devastation..." wrote Albohazen Haly. But this interpretation is more after the superstitious method of medieval Astrology than in the modern psychological, scientific manner. It is true that nothing can begin without Mars. Nor anything end. But he is no good at continuous effort. A mighty roar of raging fire, a spurt of fierce burning then...rapidly out. His action is snappy and sharp as a sword thrust...and "sword" is the operative word. For all cutting instruments come under him: knives, daggers, swords, in fact all metal that can be given a sharp cutting edge.

Mars is brutally direct, self-gratifying and inconsiderate. In Astrological terms he is a *Malefic*...a Planet whose bad influence outweighs his good. But modern Astrology, comprehending the Stars and *from them human nature* much more widely, sees in Mars the source of all energy and initiative. His Force, like all Fire and Water, must be controlled, exploited. He makes a good servant. But in the wake of his Mastership follow death, disaster and ruin.

Just as he is our fighting instinct so is he our means of self-defence. He produces leaders. And of vital significance, *none of us could survive without him*. On the other hand, as the Planet of metal and sharp instruments, he is also connected with accidents...from carelessness in the kitchen, through firearms as well as knives, and from floods, shipwreck and drowning...when in a Water Sign.

Mars then, the flamboyant, red and fiery, has rulership relating to courage and heroism as well as destruction with wounds. Unable to live *without* him, to live *with* him we must learn to control him.

The Planet Jupiter...temperate, salutary, activating...is, among many other things, the Planet who unlocks doors, pulls down obstacles, grants us the means to accomplish that which we thought impossible. He was called by the Ancients *the Greater Fortune*. He has dominion over Religion, Philosophy, Science and Law. His influence on voyagers and shipping is strongly beneficial yet is gentle of disposition. And, even as the spiritual urge seeking to transcend the material comes through him, so, too, does the compulsion to gamble, the urge to pass beyond the ordinary money-making methods.

He is The Preserver as well. Protecting us in moments of acute danger...opening parachutes, producing lifebelts, ropes...even unexpected windfalls when most needed.

There may be over-confidence, over-enthusiasm...on the premise that "the road to hell is paved with good intentions". This is more due to unrealistic appreciation of matters practical than anything else. Normally Jupiter is the Planet of judgement, of perspective and soundness. And very conventional. At his highest he likes to help the more unfortunate and often endeavours to explore the realms of Religion and Metaphysics.

At the material level he will gamble and speculate and possesses all the optimism in the world...is convinced that the jackpot is ever just round the corner. Just as his reaching out compels him on in higher things so, too, does it send him travelling, exploring, seeking, seeking the off-beat path. Wherever he is, doing what he may...usually, especially in Sagittarius, a jovial, "hail-fellow-well-met" character. Good company...as traveller or guest.

He is the Planet of bounty, of generosity and of hope. He is the Planet of expansion. And come what may, lose what we will, at least we will have a jolly good time in the process.

Saturn was considered by the Ancients to be evil. In olden times he was thought to be the highest in the heavens and during the time o Ptolemy was, indeed, the farthest known Plane in our solar system. He is considered to be the Planet of material boundaries. And thus limited He too in ancient times was Malefic...*the Grea Malefic*.

Fundamentally Saturn creates our urgent need for security, for self-preservation. Natives o Saturn are ambitious...often to an over-reaching degree. There is in him, however, a deep sense of duty, a great deal of stability, conscientious ness and responsibility. In pursuit of their goals they can be patiently hard-working and rathei servile to superiors in order to gain promotion Nothing is too troublesome for the Saturnian in his aspirations and in the efforts to attain them

Sometimes he can be indolent...greedily ambitious but lacking the ability to stay the course. He can then procrastinate, be careless and slipshod in his work, rude and bullying to those under him.

Alchabitius said of Saturn "that he is evil produces and fosters men of melancholic com plexion. He signifies profound silence, mistrus

nd suspicion..." Saturnians are often unduly
ong in developing their characters and their
areers. But then, all the attributes of age are
heirs...endurance, stability, experience—quite
requently—wisdom.

Alone he may not particularly enhance the
ubject's beauty. But he can give fine bone
tructure, a noble head...appearances that age
vell.

He, the last of the Ancients' Planets, thus
imits *but also disciplines*. He is The Teacher
nd basically just. If we learn what he endeavours to teach, if we accept the positive and
discard the negative of him, we can be brought
o stability and an enviable degree of contentment.

Uranus is a large Planet possessing five moons.
Four of these revolve in a retrograde movement
...an exception making itself apparent in the
influence of Uranus on the subject. He is often
called "The Awakener", the Planet of Revo-
lution, and it is of no little significance that the
appearance of Uranus occurred during a period
marking the beginning of the American nation
and the upheavals in France. He heralds change
...frequently followed by shock. Unpredictable,
sometimes he brings a sudden windfall, some-

times sharp and unpleasant upsetting. Although isolated he is not unduly lonely. It is simply that for the most part he exists in a world of his own and encounters difficulty in trying to share it. In many cases this strangeness signifies genius.

At ordinary level Uranus can be erratic and mixed up. Yet he makes a better leader than follower. When crossed he is obdurate and unreasonable and is subject to extremes. There seems to be no happy medium...his likes and dislikes are intensive. He will fall in love fanatically and violently. But will fall out as quickly and as violently. Uranus brings peculiar attractions to unlikely persons...love affairs, marriages, friendships are usually so intense they can hardly be expected to be sustained for long. Exciting and memorable, contact can be with Uranus, but with devastating aftermaths. The Uranian stays outside, remains beyond the normal patterns of Life. His own life is thus erratic and his relationships difficult. There tends to be a constant tension present in the life of the Uranian, a permanent frustration. The concentrated intensity, the urgency with which he undertakes everything he does, his perfectionism and preciseness can be extremely exhausting... to others.

A most original person, the Uranian.

Neptune, another of the "moderns", is also a large Planet. He influences mass movement and mass emotion. But like a storm at sea...working up slowly to an ungovernable fury. To most Neptunians everything is larger than Life and much lovelier. Like Jupiter, his motives are not evilly intentioned. Merely that much of his world is Dreamland. A kind of miasma invades situations involving him.

At the high level Neptune dispenses great sensitivity. This is often expressed through art or music and, above all, through mysticism. There is strong desire for unity...with God or man...and an escapist element. The occult, afterlife, mediumship...all have compelling fascination for Neptunians. He will martyr himself unmercifully in the expiation of sin...or imagined sin.

Neptune's action is always gentle and subtle. But nonetheless forceful and determined. No violent struggle, no perceptible transition... simply, without clash of will or noisy argument, the change has been completed. Strange, exotic in a puzzling, quiet manner, he can be most charming. But mainly, it is to be feared, looks at the world through tinted spectacles. Fortunately, Sun and Moon and Sign, by their juxta-positions or otherwise in the Zodiac, all play complementary roles in Personal Horoscopes. We now know that influences of Planets can never be wholly bad. Or, for that matter, are not invariably wholly good.

Pluto is the most recent acquisition to our Zodiac. A tiny Planet. Although appearing to be Martian in character he resembles the negative side of Mars in Scorpio rather than the flamboyant Mars in Aries. He is potently influential in uncovering the concealed, bringing the hidden things out in the open. Eruptive in action. So that the dormant, suppressed for years, can suddenly burst forth with explosive fury. There is much that is compulsive in his action and event will follow event with startling rapidity.

He often influences but very little. The exception can be when he is found in conjunction with another Planet...at which time he will give great emphasis to that Planet's action.

Many modern Astrologers associate his discovery with the rise of organised crime...gangsters, hi-jackers and bootleggers during Prohibition in the United States of America. This is not, in my opinion, good Astrology. The discovery of his existence did not mean that at that discovery his influence began. Whether or not we knew of him his influence must always have been there.

His parallel with Mars as a Planet of "beginnings and endings" is extremely marked in that the entrance of him into a Zodiacal Sign frequently ushers in some new era. Just as his exit seems to coincide with the fading of an old order.

A rebellious fellow. Most "mod". Altogether a "mixer" and a "rule-breaker".

THE ZODIAC

WE have so far learned that the first three key
to a character analysis is the position of the Sur
in the Sign at birth, the position of the Moon
and...obviously...the Sign itself. It can be seer
that if the Sun is favourably "aspected" i
represents our highest aspirations. The Sign
influencing the physical body, also strengthen
or weakens Sun's tendencies. Moon, primaril
affecting the Subconscious, effects...through th
chain of conscious Thought...action an
character. The person hesitating between Signs..
born on the Cusp...must decide for himsel
which Sign makes the stronger impact on hi
Personality. No other Astrological Rule may b
applied.

As designated by Astrologers the Zodiac is th
ecliptic made by the course of the Earth roun
the Sun plus a belt several degrees wider abov
and below it. It is roughly circular. Astrolog
divides it into 12 sections...the circle of 360
divided by 12 creating sections of 30° each

These sections are the 12 Signs of the Zodiac.

For the purpose of "measurement" the first Sign is Aries. This is because the "beginning" of the Zodiacal Year is at the Vernal Equinox... when day and night are of approximately equal length all over the world. This is on March 21st. It takes Sun until April 20th to pass through this Sign and enter Taurus on April 21st. And so on through the 12 Signs.

The Earth's rotation allows us to see the whole of the Zodiac during each 24 hours so that, Astrologically, every 4 minutes there will be a different degree of the Zodiac on the eastern horizon...The Rising or The Ascendant Sign. And at the Zenith...the highest point overhead known as Midheaven or MC.

As well as dividing the heavens into 12 the Astrologer also divided the Birth Chart into 12. These cover the various departments of Life and are The Houses of the Horoscope. The first division, generally speaking, begins from either The Ascendant or the Midheaven. These Houses correspond more or less in interpretation to that of the Signs. For example...The First House (which starts in The Ascendant) is related to Aries, the Person Himself. The Second House to Taurus...the wealth of the Person of that

Sign...etc.

It will therefore be noted that The Ascendant is determined by the time of Birth. It is The Zodiacal degree rising...ascending...in the east when we are born. It gives the *angle,* the point of view on our pattern, hence on the Life. We are then a mixture of the Signs and Planets and of Sun and Moon as they are situated at the time of our birth.

The Zodiac is yet further divided into 2 major divisions...Element and Quality. The Qualities... Cardinal, Fixed or Mutable...show how the Elements will act. In short they *qualify* them.

It is beyond the purpose of this book to attempt to enlarge on the deep technicalities of Scientific Astrology. We are mainly concerned only with Character analyses. But in passing it may be considered helpful to comprehend at least a little of the numerous complexities, the many-shaped pieces of the jigsaw, to which the Astrologer must recourse to complete his pattern.

The Elements are Fire, Earth, Air and Water. In that order. It will be seen that they follow the recognised Creative and Evolutionary patterns.

The Qualities are the levels of action on which the Signs will work. They are related to the

Seasons. The Cardinal Signs, Aries, Cancer and Capricorn mark the commencement of the new... Spring, Summer, Autumn and Winter. They coincide with the Equinoxes and Solstices.

The Fixed Signs mark the High Season, and the Mutable the transition from one Season to another.

The Cardinal Signs stand for direct action and thrive in a tough world. Cardinal Sign Subjects are often pioneers and can make snappy decisions. The best example of a Cardinal Sign is, of course, Aries...the beginning of the Zodiacal Year and the First Fire Sign.

Taurus, Leo, Scorpio and Aquarius are *Fixed* Quality Signs. They correspond with The Seasons when they have settled. For the most part they dislike change and, loosely, can be thought of as builders on the foundation laid down by The Cardinals.

The *Mutable* Signs denote. changeability. They are of critical frames of mind and tend, often, to destroy that which the *Fixed* Signs have built. They are Gemini, Virgo, Sagittarius and Pisces. They prefer talking to action. They make excellent company.

ZODIACAL CHARACTER ANALYSES

ARIES (The Ram)
March 21—April 20

Ruling Planet: Mars
Element: Fire
Quality: Cardinal
Positive
1st House
Gems: Sapphire, opal, and amber
Colour: Violet, azure and gold
Metal: Iron and gold
Signs in harmony for companionship, marriage, business: Gemini, Libra and Cancer.

In General

The First Sign of the Zodiac...*Cardinal Fire!* The aim is creation *in action.* The captain, leader, the pioneer among us ploughing the first furrow. Full of resource, enterprise and ardour, the Arietian positively enjoys overcoming difficulties and will go out of his way to challenge opposition.

Softer in "the female of the species". But

nevertheless the characteristic warmth and vitality are still displayed. The female Arietian cannot tolerate lack of enthusiasm in others. Neither does she make any bones about making her feeling on this abundantly clear. She often craves for more scope and larger opportunities for swaying her fellow creatures and, like her male counterpart, is not particularly concerned of others' opinions about her.

Aries is heroic, usually makes a courageous... if rather rash...soldier. His decisions, being hasty, do not allow for possible dangers.

There is no malice borne by the Arietian. The present being so exciting, the future so challenging, he quickly forgets the past. Hopeful, enthusiastic, optimistic...frequently aggressive... he lives vividly, seldom tranquilly.

He is a delightful person to meet; cheerful, refreshingly bright and lively. He normally relishes a good fight. But is astute enough to appreciate when to retreat...on the well-tried premise that "He who fights and runs away, lives to fight another day".

By many Astrologers he is considered to be quite a "stranger to the truth". I find this more than a little unjust. The Arietian simply is not hypocritically subtle. To the contrary he is direct to the point of bluntness, straightforward and honest. On the other hand, when he feels the necessity, his lying can be utterly convincing. Usually he does not see any point to lying...on the assumption that he has nothing of which to be ashamed.

Health of The Arietian

The Arietian is muscular, vibrating with energy and glows with good health. The movements usually are quick and impulsive and the whole personality is intensely alive. This excessively vibrant good health, with its surfeit of vitality, renders him liable to suffer from headaches, blood pressure and feverish complaints. While the headstrong compulsion to continue against all odds some enterprise or other is naturally responsible, quite often, for fits of anger and impatience. Many Arietians are also accident-prone. The remedy is obviously cultivation of patience, gentleness, forethought...and humility. The native should heed carefully the indications as shown in a Personal Horoscope.

The head is ruled by Aries...to such an extent that all the expressions connected with the word can be applied. "Headstrong," "heady," "plunging in headfirst," "getting ahead," "headache"...It is his strength and his weakness.

Success and The Arietians

The Arietian possesses within his character and range all the abilities...the determination the ardour, the enterprise and the drive...to achieve success in business or occupation *provided there is less organising and acting on behalf of other people and more self-disciplinary emphasis, more effort in channelling the abilities towards goals beneficial to himself.* While... seemingly paradoxically..."looking before leaping" he should nevertheless "have a go" take a chance, be less anxious regarding security Of an independent frame of mind, the Arietian should be...by careful application of the omens written in his Stars...the ideal pupil capable of profiting by the discipline of "living-for-today".

He is an able leader and wonderful to have around in a tricky situation. His optimism is infectious and thus boosts morale. The force of the physical nature plus the strong veins of commonsense and idealism are well blended with intellect and intuition to enable the subject to occupy positions of responsibility and trust Again...*provided the tendency to be self-willed and dogmatic can be curbed or sublimated*

38

There can be, too, dangers of living too much in the mind which, unless controlled, can lead to a degree of self-centredness and even conceit.

As the primary characteristics of the Arietian are determination and energy and he possesses fundamental ambitious urge...enthusiastic aspirations...and because he is masterful and self-reliant, there would appear to be no reason why the self-disciplined subject should not realise his or her dearest ambitions.

Friendship and Love

The emotional life of the Arietian is filled largely with enthusiastic friendships calling forth the intense warmth of his or her heart. This same impetuosity and ardour characterizes the Romance. He can be frank, generous and extremely affectionate. But impulsiveness will lead to dangerous changeability unless stronger loyalty and tenacity can be acquired. And the aggressiveness "natural" to the Martian subli- mated considerably. Then the warrior can...so often does...settle down with some admiring, gentle and adaptable mate.

By curbing the compulsion to "rush in where fools fear to tread", by cautious and thoughtfully using the Compatability Guide of the Stars there is no apparent reason why the Arietian should not find...in his passionate love...true marital happiness and contentment. In over simplification...he really needs a gentle, restraining foil to his impulsiveness. Which can be found in subjects born under the Signs of Gemini, Libra and Cancer.

Summing Up

The *positive qualities* of one born under the powerful and dominating Sign of Aries, *ruled by fiery Mars,* are leadership, grit, enthusiasm, wonderful recuperative powers...of bobbing up from defeat...and warm-heartedness.

The *negative qualities* show in recklessness, lack of tact, an element of ruthlessness, foolhardiness and a wanting in "staying power".

Some Famous Arietians

Leonardo Da Vinci: Joseph Haydn: Henry James: Vincent van Gogh: Arturo Toscanini: Harry Houdini: Charles Chaplin: Joan Crawford: Bette Davis: Tennessee Williams: Peter Ustinov: Marlon Brando.

Lucky Charms associated with subjects of Aries are few, but the Egyptian Scarab Charm, modernised in title from the ancient Khepera to "Keppa", is one. Lucky numbers, if there are such things...and many believe that there are... might well be the Planetary Positions at Birth figures.

TAURUS (The Bull)
April 21—May 20

Ruling Planet: Venus
Element: Earth
Quality: Fixed
Negative
2nd House
Gems: Jade, agate and emerald
Colours: Blue, pink
Metal: Iron or steel, gold for women
Signs in harmony for companionship, marriage, business: Capricorn, Virgo, Libra, Scorpio.

In General

Each time Sun enters a new Sign of the Zodiac there is a marked change of character. This is most prominent when it moves from Aries to Taurus. The difference is like the proverbial "chalk and cheese".

Fixed Earth! Almost self-explanatory. The Taurean possesses great stability of character and purpose, has a steadfast mind and is unhaken in adversity. The strong, silent type. Patient but also quite stubborn with a tendency to become very determined in the pursuit of desires. Tenacious, he generally excels when pushed by others...business associates, friends, wife. Astrologers feel that he has found his true position in the Universe...the Centre...identifying himself with the very heart of things. A plodder who likes the creature comforts, he is one who will work zealously to obtain and keep them. In adverse circumstances his patience and perseverance are little short of miraculous. All action is deliberate and prudent. He is long-suffering but can, if provoked beyond endurance, give way to an occasional outburst of wrath that can be dangerous for the unthinking provoker. Sensitive to the opinions of the world, he is acquisitive and feels secure when surrounded by material possessions.

His loyalty makes him a good friend, a desirable business associate and a faithful lover. It is difficult to ruffle him...with his uncomplicated make-up, joy-of-living, honesty and integrity.

Health of The Taurean

Usually well-proportioned and on a generous scale. The women of this Sign are often very

beautiful, indeed elegant, charming and graceful.
Both sexes have musical voices and opera singers
are found among Taureans in abundance.

The health can normally be considered robust.
But it can be endangered by self-indulgence...
sometimes, unless watched carefully...by glut
tony, alcoholism and sensuality.

The most susceptible part of the Taurean's
body is the throat. He seems more prone to
sickness affecting the throat...tonsilitis, laryn
gitis, quinsy, pharyngitis and colds.

He has slow but strong recuperative power
and his capacity for endurance permits him to
tolerate setbacks with equanimity...usually. It is
advisable, however, that he watch his diet and
turns his vitality always outward for the pleasure
and benefit of others rather than let it consume
him and cause morbidity. The emphasis of the
Taurean diet should be on quality rather than
quantity for, without discipline, the tendency to
put on weight will rapidly assert itself.

Success and The Taurean

His commercial integrity fits him for trustee
ship, guardianship and many kinds of publi
office. With training he can succeed in any
occupation although he is rather slow...but

44

methodical...in learning. Not necessarily over intelligent, he is nevertheless shrewd and tenacious in business. And...a valuable asset in commerce and industry...secretive when with an added ingredient of incentive.

Gambling is not one of the Taureans weaknesses. They seek firm foundations, safe, well-tried methods and prefer to be able to see the steps ahead. Conservative, devoted to detail, painstaking and unhurried. Suitable jobs can include managership...of the routine type... building, industrial, technical and statistical pursuits.

Taurus is the money Sign of the Zodiac. With his patience and endurance the Taurean...liking the comfortable home full of good furnishings... will pursue wealth diligently.

This pursuit is almost invariably accomplished honourably and with due regard to the fortunes or misfortunes of others. There can be in some cases a miserly streak which at worst is downright greedy, at best merely ensures that the subject lives well within income...however ample. Seldom is the bankrupt Taurean to be found. The incentive for hard work will always be material status. This is the standard by which he measures success.

Friendship and Love

The Taurean is exceptionally faithful in love and loyal in friendship. This loyalty will endure despite rebuff and despite a certain difficulty in comprehending that others may not...or cannot ...invariably achieve the high standards set by him.

The husband possesses all the necessary qualifications conducive to the successful marriage. In the primitive type there may appear emotional immaturity manifested in an over-amorous, sensual and violent nature. But this can be adjusted by awareness and is compensated for by the basic reliability and generosity. His exquisite taste in beauty extends beyond materialism and leads him to choose a lovely partner... whom he likes to see remain lovely and always looking attractive. Stolid and dependable...and loving to be depended upon. That is the Taurean man.

The wife responds to considerate treatment and luxurious environment. Often very beautiful she is neither conceited nor vain but is, rather, self-knowledgeable and confident. In return for her love and devotion she expects protection and affection. She gives dependability...and looks for it in her husband. She seldom doubts hi affection although beneath her facade of calm reserve she can be quite jealous. She can accept a great deal of disappointment and her sense of proportion prevents her from being *too* exacting. She will tolerate untold hardship and remain faithful. Her love of domestic life embraces an intense love of life itself...and particularly, with the *dolce vita*...the background of a good and beautiful home.

Summing Up

Positive qualities are steadfastness, conservatism, and the wonderful ability to repair the damage caused by other people's errors. The Taurean is persevering and solid. There is in the native an acute colour sense, artistic bent and dislike of strife. Incentive perpetually drives them on and on.

Negatively there can be a degree of selfishness and greed with a wide streak of obstinacy. Materialism and possessiveness, unless controlled as pinpointed by a Personal Horoscope, mar much of the make-up however fundamentally good. Intensely loyal, there can be a disturbing suspicion of others' loyalty. Again unless watched...a tendency toward indolence: in the woman, slovenliness.

Some Famous Taureans

Niccolo Machiavelli: Oliver Cromwell: Catherine the Great: Honore de Balzac: Johannes Brahms: Bertrand Russell: Lady Astor: Harry Truman: Margaret Rutherford: Fred Astaire: Gary Cooper: Salvador Dali: Queen Juliana: Yehudi Menuhin: Queen Elizabeth II: Audrey Hepburn.

Many Taureans believe that the Naga Dragon Charm of Malaya is associated with their Sign. There is little or no evidence of this that is recorded. In fact, the Naga Charm is widely believed in throughout the world, and for all Signs. All sorts of systems for arriving at Lucky numbers have been devised, but the Planetary Position Figures at a Birthdate are probably the only ones really associated with a Taurean's...or anyone else's...birth.

GEMINI
(The Heavenly Twins)
May 21—June 21

Ruling Planet: Mercury
Element: Air
Quality: Mutable
Positive
3rd House
Gems: Beryl, aquamarine and pearl
Colour: Silver and blue
Metal: Silver
Signs in harmony for companionship, marriage, business: Libra, Gemini, Aries and Aquarius

In General

Gemini, inquisitive, intellectual, eternally seeking expression, and with a disposition as changeable as British weather, the mood reacting to environment and people contacted. Charming, ambitious, sensitive, their main function is to make life more interesting for themselves and others.

The driving force of the Geminian is the ardent desire for intellectual satisfaction. Normally a brilliant and gay individual but the craving for fulfilment and the wish to influence those around him can often lead to intellectual suffering and feelings of martyrdom.

To Astrologers Gemini is "The Child of the Zodiac"...eagerly curious, inclined a little to superficiality so that he tends to be "Jack of all trades and master of none". Nevertheless the Geminian is unusually talented in all fields of learning...the humanities, the arts, languages and even gadgetry. Lack of power of concentration, however, inevitably makes for restlessness and boredom. Ruled as he is by Mercury... Messenger of the Gods...he dislikes immobility, must be on the move tirelessly. A fast and interesting talker, a quick thinker and one who learns easily and remembers clearly. The fact that he contradicts himself daily...sometimes hourly...causes him no embarrassment for by then he is pressing on, ever on, to things new. A gatherer of news, a communicator...clever, smart, nervous. The House, the 3rd, is that of Travel, Study and Relationships. But the travelling undertaken by the Geminian is seldom over great distances. In his relationships he appreciates sympathy and understanding and, above all, intellectual approbation. He does not "suffer fools gladly".

Health of The Geminian

A body as active and alert as the mind. Usually slender and lithe of figure apparently living "on the nerves". Bright, *alive* eyes...often hazel or grey. Complexion fair and quick to blush. Gemini women are usually quite fascinating...sometimes gushing. The symbolic winged sandals of Mercury represent here the winged words liberated by Geminian intellect. Appropriate, too, to the quick, nervous movements of the body and legs.

The lungs are his weak spot. Which makes him subject to colds, influenza, pleurisy and related diseases. The Geminian would be well advised to smoke as little as possible.

Success and The Geminian

It is significant that many, many financiers and tycoons are from this Sign...both men and women. Being industrious, inquisitive and cheerfully active the Geminian prefers to work where these and his intellectual capabilities are most suited. He will be found among agents,

51

merchants, bankers, brokers, lawyers, secretaries, surgeons, dentists, engineers and electronic skilled men...and women. He is excellent at buying and selling...despite being "security-minded". Ever fresh ideas for making money are sought...in the negative type by means not always strictly honest. It might be advisable for the weaker Geminian to study closely the Planetary indications when seeking employment...Jobs involving financial responsibility can afford temptation.

There is nothing mean about the Geminian. On the contrary he is usually too generous. This should be guarded against. Let the yellow... amber...which is his "warning colour" shine brightly enough to inform him that the prudent "black" of the bank account is preferable to the "red" so often incurred from gestures of foolhardy generosity.

Friendship and Love

The Geminian is gregarious, likes people around...and, being excellent company, people like him to be around. Corresponding with the 3rd House...The House of the Lower Mind...and he gravitates towards people of similar tastes and interests. In romance he seeks intellectual companionship without regard for age or condition. Obviously, this is not always obtainable and the failings give rise to flirtatious inconstancies. With the "right" partners however... indicated as "harmonious" or "compatible" by Astrology...Geminians are capable of deep loyalty and true love.

The husband requires a sharing of intellectual interests and a partner not averse to sudden change of environment. From her he needs inspiration without nagging. Pressure put upon him he finds intolerable. The wife from the House not listed as "harmonious" should be cautious.

Being an intellectual, the Gemini wife also seeks compatible mental companionship. Domesticity is secondary to her. Accomplished, she has many interests outside of the home which are time-devouring. All being equal, however, she can normally manage the home and outside affairs competently.

Summing Up

Positive qualities are the logical, analytical approach to Life and the confidence stemming from self-knowledge. The craving for diversity leads in many cases to brilliant results in experi-

mental science and other fields. Rationalism
and commonsense are great assets, as are the
charm, gaiety and optimism...and, of supreme
importance, the keen sense of humour.

On the *negative* side superficiality predom-
inates. And the factual often has priority over
the emotional. Procrastination and wavering
tortuous concentration on insignificant detai
produce their own chaos. Expedience can serve
for ethics. It is not for nothing that the Ruling
Planet of Gemini is the Patron of thieves and
vagabonds.

Some Famous Geminians

John F. Kennedy: Bob Hope: Beatrice Lillie
Marilyn Monroe: Duchess of Windsor: Duke o
Edinburgh: Laurence Olivier: Prince Rainier
Queen Victoria.

Geminians are great believers in Luck, and i
anything that can hurry it along! The Tibetai
Talli Charm, the Malayan Naga Charm and th
Egyptian Scarab, Keppa, are often all include
in the Luck-Armoury of a Geminian. They hav
no doubt about Lucky Numbers, and if ther
are any for them, and anyone else, they ma
well be the zenithal presentation of the Planetar
Positions on their Birthdate.

CANCER (The Crab)
June 22—July 23

Ruler: Moon
Element: Water
Quality: Cardinal
Negative
4th House
Gems: Jade, ruby, emerald and onyx
Colour: Violet
Metal: Silver
Signs in harmony for companionship, marriage, business: Pisces, Scorpio, Taurus, Libra, Capricorn.

In General

Not only symbolic of the thick protecting shell and the vicious claws that can nip, but...Astrologically more correct...the Sign of Motherhood, the urge to raise a family, the instinct to nourish. For Cancer...from the Latin...also denotes breast. A sensitive, sympathetic Sign, noble, kind and protective. Being a Water Sign it is active *and* emotional.

It produces shy, rather timid people who are very self-conscious. Despite being emotional the Cancerian hides his feelings dead-pannishly. But the charm of the smile reveals all that the apparent timidity conceals. Adaptable and tenacious and, like the Moon, the Sign's Ruler, shining brilliantly or suffering eclipse.

The whole gamut of emotion lies open to the Cancerian. Both past and future are as real to him as the present. Responsive to suffering he can feel, and make others feel, as no other type can. Often morbid and inclined towards melo-drama and the sensational. Liking praise and kindness but extremely sensitive to criticism. The style is picturesque and vivid. Delivering and re-delivering his message, he adapts its form while preserving the essence until he sparks off the enthusiasm he seeks.

Home is the first love of the Cancerian. Affec-tions and maternal elements are strong and marked. "Absence definitely makes the Can-cerian heart grow fonder." Early childhood memories and old ties of friendship are treasured. There are powerful strains of conventionality and conservatism...in the finest sense...about this subject while, paradoxically, he is quite interested in the novel.

Kind and gentle, people yearn to confide in him. Although of a forgiving nature, when his feelings are hurt the temper can be aroused. But not for long. It is up and out. He is responsive neither to severity nor coercion. But by and large the nature is loving, loyal, sympathetic.

Health and The Cancerian

Of a nervous disposition and susceptible to criticism to a worrying degree. A liking for candy and sweet things upsets the digestion.

The bone structure is generally the most striking feature. Limbs are long, shoulders broad, hands and feet large. Due to over-indulgence there is a proneness to excessive weight later in life.

The emotional nature is usually too strong for the physical. Symptoms can be exaggerated... leading to serious misapprehensions. Financial fear often increases the anxiety. The Cancerian can wallow in self-pity. Touchiness, gloom, bitterness and resentments must be severely dealt with to avoid bad health...physical and mental.

Success and The Cancerian

Being careful with money the Cancerian does

not tolerate dishonesty...in himself as well as in others. There are excellent chances of this type finding success in business because of this thrift and prudence. But he also makes a good school teacher...due to his tenacity of recollection. There is present a good business acumen mixed with the vital ingredients of initiative and imagination. Add the will to accomplish, and we have the makings of the very successful.

Friendship and Love

Unless disciplined, inclined to be fickle. The Cancerian is very romantic but, being sensitive to ridicule, is often too shy or proud to reveal it. In friendship nothing suits him more than to talk over old times...as an old soldier or sailor he loves the evening's yarn with old comrades. Until Mister...or Miss...Right comes along there can be many flirtatious "trial-and-error" experiments with Love. But the obsession to settle down can help the search for a person born under a harmonious Sign. This leads to a divinely contented domestic life, complete and fulfilled.

The man is seldom easy to live with. He can be most charming when he so desires but, more often, despite his love of home, can be indolent and self-indulgent. "The road to hell being paved with good intentions," he often spoils himself by naggingly interfering with household affairs. Dissatisfaction plays havoc...with him and those around him.

The wife needs protection, help and guidance. She often makes a god of her husband and can suffer the mental torments of hell when she discovers his feet of clay.

Summing Up

The stronger type...the *positive* or evolved...is capable of disciplining the emotions. He is sensitive to "atmosphere". His powerfully strong memory accompanied by vivid imagination can become valuable assets. The love of home extends to intense love of country and, naturally, a keen appreciation of tradition.

Negatively, the Cancerian, self-pitying to a hypochondriacal degree, will find himself reluctant to make the necessary effort in any required direction. He seems to enjoy a periodical wallow in imagining terrible possibilities.

The feeling for others, of which there can be abundance, may be shallow. Fulfilment is not achieved because true affection does not develop and sensationalism plays the substitute for realistic relationship.

Some Famous Cancerians

Duke of Windsor: Jean Cocteau: Gertrud
Lawrence: Nelson Rockefeller: Henry VIII
Rembrandt: Jean Jacques Rousseau: Charle
Laughton:Ernest Hemmingway:Louis Armstrong
Oscar Hammerstein II: Richard Rodgers.

Luck for the Cancerian is a very real, accepted
quality. Charms play a part in their beliefs, and
the Egyptian Scarab Charm is one that man
Cancerians believe has links with their Sign
Khepera, or Keppa, as it is now usually called
is one such presentation of this ancient talisman
As with all other Signs the only numbers...Luck
or otherwise...associated with them, astrologi
cally speaking, are the figures that give the
Positions of the Planets...zenithally will do, and
for a meridional erection...on their birthdate.

LEO (The Lion)
July 24—August 23

Ruler: Sun
Element: Fire
Quality: Fixed
Positive
5th House
Gems: Ruby, gardonyx, peridot
Colour: Orange
Metal: Gold
Signs in harmony for companionship, marriage, business: Sagittarius, Aries, Libra and Aquarius.

In General

Proud, generous, trusting, energetic, domineering, authoritative, enthusiastic, he burns steadily with ferocity until exhausted. Leo is the Royal Sign, the Sign of the Conscious Ego who feels responsible to Society for his actions and whose best action is benevolent Rulership. The *fully* developed Leonian has about him that regal bearing that makes all in his presence

61

instinctively brace themselves, square the shoulders, stand tall.

Grand...in a grand manner. Loving expensive surroundings while exuding an air of confidence and good humour that is a tonic for all.

Like his Ruler, Sun, he loves to shine, to excel...without prejudice upon whom he shines. Unlike Cancer he is neither timid nor shy. In fact, the complete extrovert. Powerful, magnetic personality, entertaining not an iota of self-doubt, he nevertheless considers it beneath him to "blow his own trumpet". As befits a King... let the court heralds sing his praises, let the Royal trumpeters sound off.

Astrologers talk of "Lucky Leo" and indeed many Leonions attribute their success in life to gigantic slices of luck. Henry Ford, a Leonian himself, did so on many a public occasion.

The Leonian seldom finds it necessary to struggle for position..."A-doing what comes naturally" seems to take him to the top. There is nothing subtle about him...his intentions are signalled quite openly. The oblique methods of the Crab are entirely alien to him. This is perhaps why he requires the admiration of his associates...his "courtiers"...to egg him on to achieve his ambitions. He prefers huge and far reaching schemes to fiddling little ones. Generally, he is magnanimous to those he defeats although he seldom forgets an insult or an affront to his pride. Yet, like the other Fire Signs, he neither bears a grudge nor seeks revenge. Disliking unpleasantness in all its forms he simply gets out of the way...if he cannot control things.

He dislikes hard work, so consequently he is a born organiser, a kind master and not a slave driver. Most underlings like him. Pleasure and the *dolce vita* is for him when he can get it. He also loves the open air and...obviously... the Sun.

Health and The Leonian

Physically, it is not easy to pass over a Leo type in a crowd. Commanding of presence, stateliness of bearing, he is often large and fair... leonine head with a mane of hair. Slow and dignified in manner. The body is symmetrical with the limbs well-proportioned. Dancers figure prominently among Leonians. Never doing things by half he is either exceptionally strong... radiating vitality...or permanently ailing. This sickness can be caused by unrequited love and /or wounded vanity.

Success and The Leonian

Ideal for the large enterprise. Multi-sided himself he understands and appreciates others' qualities. He never wastes energy and, as a leader, never expects others to do that which he would not undertake himself.

Luck usually plays a significant role in his achievements. But his alertness to opportunity allows him to take full advantage of Dame Fortune, in other words, he seldom fails to "play his Luck".

Creativeness, too, is inherent in him...creativeness on all levels of human endeavour. Children being the creation of our bodies he is fond of them. In fact, fond of all creative activities...as far-ranging as love affairs to speculating. With Leo it is most assuredly a case of brave heart winning...whether it be the fair lady or the jackpot.

Friendship and Love

Emotionally, Leonians tend to be over-generous and they frequently misplace their affections. They also are inclined to form unwise friendships. Heartaches, jiltings and broken or unhappy marriages often ensue. On the other hand, however, their big-heartedness, their magnanimity and powers of forgiveness often avert tragedy. In fact often bring incredible happiness. Nevertheless "lucky at cards, unlucky at love" can be too frequently the theme unless they match with harmonious Signs.

Summing Up

The *positive qualities* abound...infinite faith and trust in others, understanding and appreciation, possessed of unlimited organisational abilities, unbounding courage, full of energy; the list is unending.

Negatively there can be an insatiable thirst for personal glory, ambition for authority and an illusory conviction of "kingship" by giving themselves airs of grandeur and self-importance. All of which can be successfully adjusted by consulting an up-to-date Personal Horoscope.

Some Famous Leonians

Napoleon: Sir Walter Scott: Alexandre Dumas: G. B. Shaw: Henry Ford: C. G. Jung: Orville Wright: T. E. Lawrence: Mae West: Aldous Huxley: Henry Moore: Ogden Nash: Dag Hammarskjold: Jacqueline Kennedy: Princess Margaret.

Subjects of Leo are often hard-hearted, but they believe in Luck all right. They favour, among Charms, the Egyptian Scarab, Keppa... possibly because of its connection with Egypt, the Sun (their Ruler) and its vast antiquity. They also use the Malayan Dragon Charm, Naga, and sometimes, if they are travellers, the Kiki Charm. Their Lucky Numbers may well be the Positions of the Planets, zenithally, on their Birthdate.

VIRGO (The Virgin)
August 24—September 23

Ruling Planet: Mercury
Element: Earth
Quality: Mutable
Negative
6th House
Gems: Sapphire, chrystolite or diamond
Colour: Grey or navy blue
Metals: Gold
Signs in harmony for companionship, marriage, business: Capricorn, Taurus, Virgo, Aries and Pisces.

In General

"Honour thy father and thy mother" could well be the motto of the Virgonian. Everything is tested in the furnace of criticism with discrimination but the bias of intense loyalty remains. The Ministering Angel caring for parents...and others...selflessly.

Ruled as she is by Mercury she possesses a

high degree of intelligence which co-ordinates perfectly with physical talents...usually of the hands.

The Virgonian is a perfectionist, concerned with minute details tidily pigeon-holed. Large issues tend to overwhelm. Strict attention to the rules is tempered with judgement and wisdom in which feeling seldom interferes. The ability to get straight to the point often offends...although, generally, the Virgonian is reasonably easy to get on with. He...and, of course, she...is splendidly competent and, but for a disinclination to be troubled about original causes, quickly appraises a situation and perceives the smoothest way to see it through.

Success in literature, criticism and the arts is the considered norm of the Virgonian. But she is a practical-minded maid of Earth whose feet never leave the ground. Fanciful ideals offend her commonsense. Chaste, pure, fastidious, fond of flowers, occasionally shows in herbs and healing with a fine mind which nevertheless appreciates the simple things of life.

Even tempered and slow to anger usually. But can be roused. Finds forgiveness difficult...and can bear malice for a long, long time.

Some Astrologers feel that this Sign is a selfish

ne. If this is so it is the kind of selfishness emanding perfection. Most Virgonians devote heir lives to the service of others...often for nadequate recompense. They give ungrudgingly f time, strength and ability. But when demands pon them become too unreasonable and excessive they are not afraid to say, "No!" And nean it.

Health and The Virgonian

They are usually strong and muscular and apable of great endurance. Wiry...and mostly xceedingly handsome. Regularity of features nd fineness of form give them beauty rather han plastic grace. Virgo is a healthy sign. The hief dangers to this health can be the tendencies ɔ overwork and an obsessive absorption with etail. There is a certain amount of scepticism n the make-up. Seldom serious illness. They are enerally fastidious over the purity of their food ..including the hygiene of its preparation and ooking and serving.

Success and The Virgonian

An ideal association on a board of directors vould be that in which the Virgonian served as ecretary...doing the hardest work more or less

69

thanklessly. Failure in his duties could quit
often result in the firm's business disintegrating
But not always does he necessarily work ur
appreciated. Tireless industry, practicality an
acumen cannot always go unrewarded. Th
women from this Sign are originally adept wit
the most extraordinary materials in handicraft:
They possess innate taste and dress well...ur
ostentatiously. A puritanical streak tends to ru
through the Sign. Altogether a good busines
associate and logical friend.

Friendship and Love

The heart, not melting easily, glows with
pure heat when at last it finds Love's fire:
There is hardly another Zodiacal Sign possessin
such loyalty, discrimination and reliability. Th
Sign is unmatched in its propensity for giving.
love, affection, care, well-being. Both sexe
make conscientious parents. And, though high
developed, both sexes can accept celibacy wit
equanimity...provided they are permitted t
serve their generation.

Virgonians do not like to be alone. Rathe
they like to surround themselves with intelliger
companions. As lovers, they are considerat
attentive and quite engaging. The men ar

eldom promiscuous...exceptions like Charles II *roving* the rule. The women are chaste and ure, delicate and refined, studious and, in manner at least, modest and unassuming. But t heart she is often a snob. Her critical ability nables her to sift the "chaff from the wheat". he puritanical streak ensures that she prefers he straightforward legality of uncomplicated marriage to anything precarious. Misfortune in ove will force her into a career...where she will nd refuge in her one panacea of hard, grinding ork.

umming Up

Positive qualities are exactness, discrimination, hastity, intelligence and a methodical, indus-ious approach to life. The steady qualities call orth admiration and respect. There is a high egree of fulfilment and accomplishment... irgonians go farther than others through atience, care of detail and ingenuity.

The *negative qualities,* humourless wit, sharp riticism and over-discrimination. If, as has een said, critics are creative failures, then irgonians are the most critical...captious and ard to please. Where the developed Virgonian ever seeks praise the primitive never gives it.

Prejudice and limited point of view can be failings. Perfectionism can turn to obsession with detail that will be tedious and boring. Priggishness, too...unless watched carefully... will warp the Personality, make it hypocritical and arrogant. The positive qualities will tussle here...producing inner conflict. Recourse to a Personal Horoscope can assist the subject to adjust.

Some Famous Virgonians

Queen Elizabeth I: Savonarola: Goethe: J.P. Morgan: Maurice Chevalier: John Gunther: Christopher Isherwood: William Saroyan: Leonard Bernstein: D. H. Lawrence: Sophia Loren: Greta Garbo.

A traditionally associated Lucky charm for Virgonians is the Confucius Charm, called these days the Kiki Charm...though nobody seems quite to know why. It is a charm connected with travel. Many Virgonians equally swear by the Egyptian Scarab Charm in its various representations. If Lucky numbers are a quest of a Virgonian, perhaps the only numbers associated with them are, as for all other Signs, those figures that give the zenithal Position of the Planets on their Birthdate.

LIBRA (The Balance)
September 24—October 23

Ruling Planet: Venus
Element: Air
Quality: Cardinal
Positive
7th House
Gems: Jade, opal, tourmaline
Colour: Indigo blue
Metal: Copper or gold
Signs in harmony for companionship, marriage, business: Aries, Sagittarius

In General

  A Cardinal Airy Sign that is alert, just, artistic, painstaking, honourable, *well-balanced,* affectionate and very sympathetic. Action is in the sphere of *relationships.* The Libran's power is in his deep concentration, his intensity of application and in the coolness of the mentality. There are splendid spurts of work followed by sheer, *enjoyed* relaxation. Bickerings and jealousies play no part in the Libran's life. They are too fond of beauty and concord...and justice. On the other hand the Libran, usually pleasant, full of guile and charm, and able to see both sides of the question, likes friends and acquaintances to fully agree with him. In this there are no half measures..."Those not for are 'agin'." And the disagreement can lead to enmity. Apart from this Libra seeks fulfilment through union. Like the Balance that is the Sign's symbol the Libran continually weighs the pros and cons. And weighs them with keen, subtle intelligence. There is a hatred of all things ugly. The Libran is usually surrounded with beautiful things, agreeable people. Pleasantness rather than unpleasantness is the order of the day. This can create a fair-weather kind of friendship. Misfortunes...of others...cause distress. And there is a tendency for the subject to leave the scene.

Libra can be self-willed, would like to get it all his...or her...own way. To achieve this the Stars have given endowments of charm and guile, an ability to smooth over difficulties persuade and cajole. An excellent middleman the Libran.

He is as many-sided as the Leonian, often

inds difficulty in choosing a profession. But the courtesy, painstaking patience and desire for perfection offsets this to a very great degree.

The innate strength of the Sign consists of the well-balanced element predominant in character make-up. Just themselves, they hate injustice. Honourable, they despise dishonesty. Meticulously fair, they scorn unfairness.

Health and The Libran

Inclined to plumpness and rounded curves but not, usually, to excessive fatness, the Libran has an instinct for sane health. Well nourished, the Libran appears, but sometimes the resistance to disease can be low...although response to treatment is good. Kidneys, spine and loins are weak spots but the inherent caution usually helps guard against abuses of laws appertaining to them. When frustrated there is an inclination to become depressed.

Venus ruling, as might be expected, the Personality projects kindliness and contentment. Librans are full of fun, good-looking in a refined, elegant way...lithe, graceful bodies, regular features, delicately formed hands and feet. The women are exceedingly beautiful...many Astrologers have it that they are the most beautiful in

the world. In manner they are calm and gentle...
with sweetness of voice. They love the pretty and
ornamental. Although they like to surround
themselves with interesting people they will
choose those less brilliant than themselves. They
dislike rivalry.

Success and The Libran

The impossible comes the possible. Among
those born under Libra will be found specialists
in all the professions...and, of course, many
judges. The intense capacity for sustained work,
the sensitivity and the flexibility, the shrewdness
and ingenuity make for a good partner. Libra
does not like to work alone although, as a
strategist...many generals are born under the
Sign...often the vital decisions must be made
alone. They make excellent wholesalers and
middlemen. But can also be very creative...
excelling in story-writing, play-writing, musical
composition and designing. In chemistry, too,
Librans shine brilliantly, as in all kinds of research. The Libran is not renowned for holding
on to his wealth...spontaneous generosity and
love of luxury plus social leanings can prove
costly. In short, the Libran...unless forewarned
and forearmed...can be extravagant. Para

doxically, possessing mathematical prowess, there *does* persist throughout the Sign an astonishing shrewdness that proves most useful. They will not be put upon financially. This mathematical skill makes of them competent economists. At which their indomitable energy spurs them relentlessly for the periods necessary and their ability to relax gives them the required breathing spaces.

Friendship and Love

Love is normally the most important thing in the Libran's Life. It seldom loses interest even in old age. There is a tendency towards early marriage. The man makes an excellent husband... affectionate, considerate, passionate and very, very tender. There exists a love of social life and hospitality. Home life is gracious...with the man appreciating refinement and elegance as much as the woman.

The woman likes the tough, *masculine* man... and makes an ideal wife. Her whole being revolves round her husband...sometimes to such an extent that the children seem to come off second best. But *it is* the Sign of Cardinal Air ruled by Venus, the Sign of marriage and partnership. Ruled by the Goddess of Love. The woman however likes change. This is usually managed by a tactful arrangement of ringing the changes on the social set. She is a wonderful mental companion. On all counts, however, the Balance must be preserved. Courtesy must be repaid. Division in all things is scrupulously fair. She has a beaming smile, is tender and gentle...often rather shy...is attractively sweet, in manner and in voice.

Summing Up

Libra is the Seventh House in the Horoscope. Many politicians and statesmen have planets in it. It portrays human relationship. This is a prime *positive quality* of the Libran. A strong, useful ability to see other people's points of view, impartiality, sense of fair play, integrated, *well-balanced* Personality. Add to these sympathetic understanding, charm...and how to use it...a love of harmony, a noble gentleness, a sweet disposition, you have the Libran at his...or her...best.

These positives...overdone...turn to unfortunate *negative qualities*. The partiality to divide equally can develop...or rather deteriorate...into the unpleasant "divide and rule". Perfectionism taken to extremes becomes a sickness. Sweetness and the desire for well-being become weakness and compliance. Maintaining Balance results in lack of direction. To compromise the Libran will lie. Possessiveness takes the place of true affection. Love of change can lead to boredom. It is a positive Cardinal Sign corresponding with Autumn. And Autumn, the Fall, when Summer and Winter are held in Balance, can be divinely beautiful...or bleak and ugly. Depending on one's point of view, one's approach to the acceptability or non-acceptability of Life.

Some Famous Librans

Brigitte Bardot: Sarah Bernhardt: Franz Liszt: Horatio Nelson: P. G. Wodehouse: Eleanor Roosevelt: T. S. Eliot: Dwight D. Eisenhower: William Faulkner: George Gershwin: Thomas Wolfe: Graham Green: C. P. Snow.

Librans, generally, have little or no time for "Luck". Those that do tend to believe embrace the charm they can gain belief in. None but the Egyptian scarab has achieved any connection with Librans. Lucky numbers are unlikely to be part of Libran belief, but if they feel that there must be some numbers connected with their destiny, they may well be the zenithal Planetary Position figures for their Birthdate.

SCORPIO
(The Scorpion)
October 24—November 22

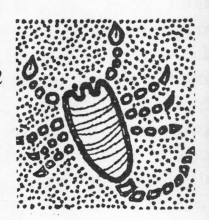

Ruling Planet: Mars
Element: Water
Quality: Fixed
Negative
8th House
Gems: Topaz, malachite
Colour: Deep red, gold or ultramarine
Metal: Steel
Signs in harmony for companionship, marriage, business: Cancer, Pisces, Leo and Virgo.

In General

The change as the Sun enters Scorpio is sharp and drastic. We now come upon an intensely serious and concentrated outlook. The highest achievement of the kingdom of Scorpio is that most difficult task of all...absolute mastery over Self. Scorpio is Fixed Water...the Sign of emotional intensity, emotion manifesting through Will.

It is the Sign of Birth, Death and Regeneration. It signifies the destruction of Ego, the domination of Desire, the abolition of all that holds back the Highest in Man. The lower nature is defeated in battle for the sake of the higher. Strong and silent, the Scorpionian has immense powers of physical attraction. A Fixed Sign, he can demand unconditional obedience from underlings and womenfolk...and often obtain it.

Scorpio, ruled by Mars, is masculine. Together with the feminine Taurus...under the rulership of Venus...they form what is known to Astrologers as the Flesh Axis. Taurus is fond of good food and wine while Scorpio revels in the power of sex...but frequently sublimates it to an extraordinarily constructive degree. There is a strong instinct to destroy in Scorpio and the "sting in his tail" seems forever seeking the weak chink in others' armour. Of caustic tongue...again instinctive and automatic...he is often astonished to discover that he has given offence. The Scorpionian plays his cards very close to the chest and is excellent at "weighing up" character. Often, the subject is powerfully psychic...without always being aware of it. Like his opposite Sign Taurus he is possessive and can undergo indescribable torments of jealousy...usually unnecessarily. He is relentless in his effort to destroy those who have incurred his enmity. Many members of the feuding Mafia are born under this Sign. But hard though he is on others he is every bit as hard on himself and drives himself with Spartan severity.

Life is a very serious affair to the Scorpionian. He identifies himself closely with whatever he is doing. Achievement is the most satsifying thing he can experience...and is vitally necessary to his self-respect. He dislikes change. And is definitely an "all-or-nothing" individual.

Health and The Scorpionian

Scorpio interests himself...and with deep understanding...in Death. He has rulership over the genitals and the bladder. The primitive type is often emotionally immature and takes exaggerated pride in his potency.

The Scorpionian is most often dark with narrow eyes and straightish eyebrows. He is sturdy...exceptionally thin and inclined to be ascetic; at least in looks...virile, well developed. Normally robust. The woman despises other women who evade marriage and motherhood. If deprived of these herself she can become terribly frustrated, completely lost as to where to direct her explosive energy and her domineering will.

Success and The Scorpionian

Absolute success in all he sets out to achieve is a "must". Ruled by the red, martial Mars, and ruling the Eighth House...that of Inheritance and Money as well as Birth, Death and Regeneration...there runs a strongly vibrant core of fierce pride which drives the subject perpetually up and on. Destroying egoism, mastering desire, obtaining rigid self-control are the obsessional aims. On top of this, being inherently unselfish, he not only wishes progress for himself, but for others as well and will give generously of his powers to assist the development of all. Astrologers thus find in this Sign a magnetic pull towards medicine. The ideal Scorpionian can indeed be equated with the ideal doctor...he being possessed of the innate power, the resolution to overcome suffering and death. Plus the strength of will to quieten the most truculent of patients.

These characteristics also make for good detectives. In this their psychic power...unconscious though it might be but usually healthy and sane...makes for speedy accuracy, observation and perception.

This intensely satisfying feeling for dominance can extend to conquering the forces of nature. Therefore the Scorpionian will make an excellent engineer of the practical kind where originality is not demanded so much as adroitness in utilizing other people's inventions.

The Scorpionian will "do or die in the attempt". None will make greater sacrifices for himself and others and he will concentrate intently on the matter in hand. He is thorough, is seldom a "Jack of all Trades"...more often the expert within his own limits. Careful in money matters...and thrifty...loves to hoard. Being secretive he prefers secretive occupations. Patriotic espionage appeals very strongly to him. As does psychology...especially psychoanalysis. In other walks of life he will be found among butchers, undertakers and all trades dealing with mortality.

Friendship and Love

These are intense and usually exclusive...with sudden antipathies and strong likes. There is little softness and sentimentality. Like all rough diamonds there can be difficulty in self expression. The heart is not worn on the sleeve. And yet there can be undue impulsiveness which iberates utterances of warmth...frequently more warm than the situation warrants.

The Scorpionian...male or female...is not an easy person to match. Too exacting, difficult to live with, demanding of others the high standards he...or she...sets and adheres to. The Scorpionian mates well with his own Sign or with someone from Cancer.

Possessing the powers of concentration that she does the woman from Scorpio makes the finest housewife and cook in the world. But having found the way to the man's heart she will often...unless he is of her own Sign or of those in harmony...inadvertently break it...temporarily...by caustic criticism. The unfortunate husband who drops cigarette ash on the perpetually vacuumed carpet will not forget it in years.

On the other hand there is little danger of the Scorpionian of either sex ruining Life by hasty engagement or ill-considered marriage.

Summing Up

Energetic and independent, passionate and determined. These are *positive qualities*. Can be priestly or make wonderful doctors because of the possession of extraordinary patience offsetting the impulsiveness. Concentration is intense. The will to dominate...in the evolved and developed...can be healthily constructive and useful to the community. The influence o Mars with the emphasis on sharp knives and cutting instruments tends to be challenged by Scorpio towards peaceful professions like surgery and butchery. The emotions are strictly con trolled. The Scorpionian definitely places "Mind above Matter".

Negatively, ever wobbling or wavering, when bad he can be very, very bad. Where other might feel mildly perturbed he will "go off the deep end" and give way to rebellious ferocious ness, jealous hatred and unbearable resentment Courageous, passionate, if he fails at self contro he may turn to drink, drugs or compulsive gambling. He simply will not take second place to anyone. The inflation of ego bursts all bounds Where discovery of other people's weaknesse occurs there can arise an unhealthy sense of self esteem. Others' failures convince him of his own successes. Recourse to a properly cast Horoscope can alert the primitive Scorpionian to such dangers, can assist adjustment and developmen so that the weaknesses, the *negatives,* can b made *positive,* can become strengths of character

Some Famous Scorpionians

Martin Luther: Marie Antoinette: Marie Curie: Pablo Picasso: Katherine Hepburn: Billy Graham: Princess Grace (Kelly): Vivien Leigh.

The boldness of some subjects of Scorpio leads them to embrace the mystical and the metaphysical, and charms play a large part in their beliefs...in the beliefs of *some* of them, anyway. They tend towards the Malayan Naga charm, the beautiful Dragon charm associated with gamblers and those others who have a deep and abiding faith in talismans and charms being able to influence chance. Those of Scorpio avidly seek Lucky Numbers, and again it should be reiterated that *if* they have any lucky numbers of any special significance for them they can perhaps only be the figures that give the zenithal positions of the Planets on their Birthdate.

SAGITTARIUS
(The Archer)
November 23—December 22

Ruling Planet: Jupiter
Element: Fire
Quality: Mutable
Positive
9th House
Gems: Jade, topaz, turquoise and zircon
Colour: Light blue
Metal: Silver
Signs in harmony for companionship, marriage, business: Aries, Leo, Sagittarius, Libra and Gemini.

In General
   A Mutable, Fiery Sign containing insatiable curiosity, intellect of high standard, impulsive and candid nature. Virtues indeed, and but part. There is also an abundance of generosity and candidness in the make-up plus a deep love of nature and sport, a quickness of under-

standing, foresight and imagination.

Unlike the Spartan and determined Scorpio Sagittarius is cheerful and hopeful...with good reason; things come easily to him. "Healthy and wise" and "happy go lucky". Of Fire, Mutable, the path lies in the creative world of ideas and thought. Boundless optimism enables the Sagittarian to disregard failure and to set sights immediately on something new. He has extraordinary mental activity, and upon everything concerning him...and not concerning him...he brings reason to bear.

The symbol is The Archer. But he is also the mixed realist...with both feet planted firmly on the ground while his head is often in the clouds.

Bringing the principles of the Sagittarian down to ordinary level we can say that by and large he is a jolly and pleasant companion. The mind is full of ideas which he will offer to all and sundry. He is broadminded, likes to do many things all at the same time, is tolerant and ruthful and abounding in bubbling humour. Like all Mutables, he is not so good in action as in thought because he lacks concentration. Ideas crowd upon him rapidly...perhaps too rapidly. He shoots at many targets. If he scores a bull's-eye he is usually too busily engaged to notice...

therefore whatever fruits may be forthcoming usually accrue to someone else.

He is fond of a good gamble and cannot take repeated failure as the Red Light. Generous to a fault he will share to the last penny and, unafraid of the future, never thinks of poverty. Casual in money matters, openhanded, he also expects others to be as generous as he is.

Jupiter rules the Sign however and influences the money and make-up to such a degree as to give the subject a duality which can make Life extremely contradictory...the jolly beggar convinced of tomorrow's windfall or the priestly intercessor on behalf of the jolly beggar who has just stolen the squire's prize cockerel. Of immense faith...in God, human nature and himself. A prophet, teacher and philosopher, in fact, of all things tending to increase Life's understanding. In all the interests taken up there will be a thorough gathering of all the necessary information.

The love of nature tends to instil a dislike of urbanity while his closeness to nature can make him a keen sportsman...fisherman, huntsman, golfer and all pastimes of the open air. A great traveller too...the farther and more remote the better. Thus making a keen explorer with a compulsive desire to embrace all the farflung outposts of the world within the sphere of his knowledge, and by actual contact, not by books. He literally enjoys the "hard lines" of rugged travel.

As if all this were not sufficient he is also endowed with a keen sense of justice. Of the Ninth House, that of the Higher Mind, he feels qualified to dispense the things of the Higher Mind...including justice, fair play, learning.

Health and The Sagittarian

Life is always worth living for the Sagittarian. Although the faint influence of Uranus can introduce slight contradictions Jupiter is far too strong and the lively humour, the happy and cheerful disposition simply cannot be suppressed. This buoyance lends itself to glowing health. The weak spots are the hips and liver... with the risk of arthritis and stiffening hips. Sagittarius endows a finely shaped head with broad brow, a frank, open countenance. The subject can be tall and thin...walking as though on stilts...while others are round of face. All have bright, restless eyes and are notable for the quick movements of body and an inclination to use hand gestures. They can be vividly expressive but not particularly graceful. Socrates depicts the plain, "egghead" Sagittarian while Jove represents the more generally accepted type. Many Spaniards portray much that is Sagittarian ...pride and independence, buoyancy of spirit, emotionalism and nervous restlessness.

Success and The Sagittarian

With his insatiable curiosity and his unflagging mental energy he makes a fine, philosophic instructor...better with older pupils or students than with the younger. These tendencies also incline him towards the legal profession...the Bar in particular. Should he choose medicine he will make a brilliant brain specialist. The Ninth House can induce him to interest himself in questions of religion and related subjects...or can show a propensity for gambling and sport. The ideal Sagittarian *would not* make a good bookmaker...he would be too inclined to gamble himself. Failing the financial resources to travel as explorer he would join one or the other of the Services and quickly volunteer for "Overseas". The restrictions of such a life would soon bore however. It is quite feasible that he would desert and make his way to remote parts.

In this country he could well be financially

interested in field sports...owning and hiring out fishing and shooting rights. The Sagittarian is often quite well off...and not mean. Jupiter symbolising "expansion" and the Sign giving intuition, the subject will embark on large projects where financial success seems reasonably assured. This intuition fits the Sagittarian ably for stockbroking...but not for dabbling himself ...intuition often being swamped by the compulsion to "have a go" far beyond rational bounds. Contradictorily it would seem...and the Sign is a mass of contradictions...later in Life, when the subject has "settled down", money can come... lots of it...from investment.

Generally speaking of the Sagittarian, whether feeling himself called to teaching or preaching, writing or exploring, advertising or bricklaying, the cheerful, likable disposition will ensure commensurate success. Happiness will always be more important than wealth. But the two can go very well together. Hence one of the occupations most suited to the Sagittarian is that of high class sales representative...especially if this calls for extensive travel abroad.

Friendship and Love

"Variety is the spice of Life." This the

93

Sagittarian brings to friendship...finding and making friends among all classes of society. Although impulsive he is not deceived by insincerity. At times open and free of speech there are occasions when reticence and inhibition clamp down.

Impulse often plays a big part in Romance... manifesting itself in the sudden attachment which rapidly cools. There can be a great many disappointments and, even when won, the Sagittarian can be difficult to hold. The taste for freedom dies hard...normally only with the subject. The husband is generally a talented man requiring a wise and diplomatic wife. Domesticity is not really for him...sport and other outside activities call too strongly. Plus the intense love of humanity. The woman, too, likes the open air. But makes a competent wife in that, unsuspicious herself, she is trustworthy, possesses mature judgement and can ignore...for the most part...the husband's outside attractions. The Sign is most suited to the Sign, so that beyond-the-hearth activities can be joint affairs.

Summing Up

On the *positive* side the chief characteristic of the Sagittarian is the extraordinary power of his intellect. Eager and curious about human welfare he is ideally suited for educationally nurturing the undergraduate...preferably in philosophy or religion. A likable, pleasant character...frank, charmingly impulsive, generous with a love of sport and nature.

Negatively...impatient, neurotic, lazy and boastful. Often cruelly inconsiderate. There can be an inclination to exaggerate...the caught tiddler will be a gigantic salmon, the missed pigeon a brace of pheasant, *ad nauseam*. Promises, the fulfilment of which is dubious, come easily to a glib tongue. Flattery can become second nature. What in the evolved can be considered enthusiasm takes on, in the primitive, careless extravagance. The love of a "flutter" can develop...or deteriorate...into compulsive gambling, and disastrously. The gay pleasantness can negatively be exhibitionism. All unlikable traits which can, quite easily, be remedied by Astrology.

Some Famous Sagittarians

Ursula Bloom: King George IV: Mary, Queen of Scots: Winston Churchill: Noel Coward: Walt Disney: Mary Martin: Julie Harris: Mark Twain: Beethoven.

Sagittarians have more of the gambling instinct than many other Signs of the Zodiac... and consequently they believe in Charms, and plenty of them! For anyone who believes in Luck as they do, the Egyptian Scarab, Khepera (keppa, as it is usually called these days) is a must. Naga, the Malayan dragon charm believed in throughout the world by people who like to flirt for the attentions of Luck, is another in the armoury of those of Sagittarius. Lucky numbers are sometimes a life-long quest for the Sign of Sagittarius's subjects. They *might* find them in the figures giving the zenithal Positions of the Planets on their birthdate.

CAPRICORN
(The Goat)
December 23—January 20

Ruling planet: Saturn
Element: Earth
Quality: Cardinal
Negative
10th House
Gems: White onyx, moonstone
Colour: Green, violet, purple and brown
Metal: Silver or Gold
Signs in harmony for companionship, marriage, business: Taurus, Virgo, Cancer, Aries

In General
    The pessimistic slogger expecting not a single "lucky break" who gets there just the same. A grave person, a responsible person with a decidedly melancholy outlook he is nonetheless ambitious...ambitious and persevering, reserved

and diplomatic. He takes Life very earnestly, anticipates the worst, manages by dint of hard work to acquire the best.

Cardinal Earth...expressing himself through materialistic action...rules by Saturn...the Planet of boundaries and material success. It is the Sign of the Administrator...in all walks. Possesses expert knowledge of the past with a profound appreciation of the present. He is difficult to analyse but there will always be found high manifestation of concern with humanity expressed in noble ambition and amazing adaptability to environment. Like The Goat, the Symbol, he climbs steadfastly and with tenacity. Up, up, forever up. Following the path trodden by successful predecessors convinced, justifiably, that "there is room at the top" for him.

All the "C's" seem to apply to the Capricornian...positively and negatively; charm, concentration, conscientiousness, conservatism, care for other...and their opinions...sensitive of criticism. Respecting authority he prefers to observe the rules. Has the "patience of Job"... will wait years to arrive. There is nothing impulsive about Capricorn. He seldom develops until his forties. Insecurity is his dread.

Health and The Capricornian

In appearance the Capricornian is usually swarthy, of leaden looks, has lank, black hair. Yet he can be an entertaining talker.

Slow to develop he becomes strong as an adult with an abundance of stamina. Exceedingly active and inclined to longevity. The bones... especially the knees...including much bowing of in the upward climb...are ruled by Capricorn. At the top he discovers a Higher Power to Whom the bowing of the knee means but little. Low content of calcium may affect the teeth. The health suffers from too much anxiety.

The woman is youthfully attractive...and maintains it for a very long time. In many cases she has the sort of beauty that definitely improves with age...has the happy knack of "ageing graciously".

Success and The Capricornian

Reputation means a great deal to him. Unafraid of hard work the way up for "The Goat" is a grind and is tortuous even though the path has been trodden before. Success is the goal and nothing is too laborious, too hard or too boring on the journey. The path may well be that of scholarship, diplomacy, social legislation or welfare. But the acquisition of wealth is normally a major part of the ambition. And the consolidation of it and all resources perpetually pesters the mind.

He excels often in building, engineering, all technical handicrafts as well as in poetry, music, religion and philosophy. In all these the traditional and conventional method...in other words, the well-tried...is preferred to the untried experimental.

Friendship and Love

The tendency to give priority to externals inclines the Capricornian to cultivate...and "bow the knee to"...persons of superior social status. Snobbery is a weakness he seldom overcomes even when ultimately successful.

In matters of love he is terrifyingly conscious of the difference in sex. In youth this leads to awkwardness in approach...often covered by conversations teeming with innuendo and a tendency to flirt. Career is invariably more important than the opposite sex however. So much so that the husband or wife is usually complementary...that is, helpful and of benefit to the career.

The Capricornian does not as a rule marry

either in haste or at a young age. There is much selectiveness about choosing the "right one". Once married, great dignity is given to the sanctity of wedded life. Underneath the facade of reserve and lack of emotion, though, there is an ardent desire for warmth and affection. It is best for the Capricornian to marry someone lively, exciting and interesting...someone from Taurus or Sagittarius or Gemini.

Summing Up

The *positive qualities* of patience, perseverance and reliability are of infinite worth by any standards. As is the earnest application to Life and its problems. The fine historic sense, the love of tradition, the enthusiastic support of authority, all are fine qualities to garnish the ambitious determination. Adaptability allows the subject to tackle successfully almost any job. Hard work is an incentive rather than deterrent. Consideration for others, a willingness and strength to help those weaker, are revealed in the evolved type.

But when life is approached by too conventional yardsticks the compelling desire to "get on" can be held back by this "not-with-it" attitude. Anxiety about the future, an inability

to "live for today" can cause unnecessary worry
frustration, even sickness. The longing for hig
standing, the servile knee-bending will nauseat
others...more especially the very people abov
who the subject is trying to placate. The innat
snobbery gets out of control. By being too stanc
offish, too severe, the chances of meeting inter
esting and useful people are lessened. The desir
for security deteriorates into a permanent feelin
of insecurity and is worsened by fear of ridicule
Parsimoniousness takes the place of prudence
Diplomacy is displaced by deceit, reserve b
furtiveness.

The secret of peace of mind was unfolde
long, long ago by a philosopher who also studie
Astrology..."know thyself". To this day ther
is not a better method of self-knowledge than
study of the Stars, with the subsequent aware
ness of weaknesses which can trip us up. Wher
possessing such knowledge, catastrophe ca
often be averted.

Some Famous Capricornians
Joan of Arc: Cecil Beaton: Cary Gran
Marlene Dietrich: Ethel Merman: Danny Kaye
Ava Gardner.

The Capricornian would *like* to believe in luck, seldom does. If he feels a charm is necessary to his chances, then he may discover a connection between Capricorn and the ancient Tibetan "Talli" charm, gently believed in throughout the East, less known here. It is believed to have arrived in the West via the exodus from Tibet of the Dalai Lama some years ago. In the East it is considered a "money-magnet". If the Capricornian has any Lucky Numbers associated with him or her, then they may be the only numbers that are, astrologically speaking, associated with their Birthdate...the figures that give the zenithal Positions of the Planets on their Birthdate.

AQUARIUS
(The Water Bearer)
January 21—February 19

Ruling Planet: Saturn
(with faint Uranian
influence)

Element: Air
Quality: Fixed
Positive
11th House
Gems: Sapphire, opal, amber and garnet
Colour: Violet and azure
Metal: Uranium and Platinum
Signs in harmony for companionship, marriage, business, Aries, Gemini, Libra and Cancer

In General

This change from Capricorn is not so startling as most other transitions. This, of course, is because both Signs are ruled by Saturn. Both are rather cold-natured, both...in their different ways...are ambitious. There would seem to be a contradiction in that Aquarius is Fixed Air...

104

and air cannot really be fixed. Which explains the subject's temperament...fixed in ideals once they are established but prone to sweeping changes of world opinion in thought and ideas.

Aquarius always seems to me the most interesting Sign in the Zodiac. The Sign of Power of the Intellect, the Sign which, while conferring capable ability, also confers modesty and sensitivity. The main characteristic of the Aquarian is breadth of vision. Unbiased and maintaining an open mind he is without any kind of prejudice. It is also the Sign of social conscience. The Water Bearer symbolizes appropriately the Life's mission of the subject...to serve, to fertilise by pouring water for the benefit of mankind. It represents the Brotherhood of Man.

He is willing to learn, equally willing to pass on what he learns. Not being emotional his feeling for suffering mankind is a matter of principle. Rather than give service to the individual he prefers bringing pressure to bear legislatively. His love of justice is for all humanity and not for just one being. The earnest desire is to change the whole world. Sympathising with the poor, feeling for the ignorant, there follows the sincere ambition to eliminate both poverty and ignorance. There is, too, a strong vein of unpredictability running through the Aquarian manifested in a rare unattachment of clinical observation...of everything and everybody. A strange but alluring mixture...seeming to be aloof and concerned, conventional and eccentric, conservative and progressive. Completely devoid of vanity and self-conceit concerning knowledge yet emphatically individualistic and unordinary.

Health and The Aquarian

Often extremely noble in appearance... especially in profile. Usually tall and fair, their voices are gentle, they possess...and can use... winning, delightful smiles. The physical movements are as leisurely as the mind...giving the impression of serenity and tranquillity. Though delicate of build there is inherent a great resistance to disease. They are fastidiously clean.

The weak points are the calves and ankles... a tendency to sprain and break the ankle exists. Diet must be watched and vitamins will offset the nervousness to which the subject can be prone. Usually of placid disposition with the wonderful ability to view things objectively.

Success and The Aquarian

A truth-seeker, neither militant nor aggresive,

he can make a very fine scientist. He never in any circumstances chooses a dull occupation. Work is agreeable to him and agrees with him. Much can be accomplished in a short space of time and with little energy. A capable individual not particularly amenable to discipline as an underdog. An inventive brain seeking the unusual. Makes a good writer, law-maker, innovator in all kinds of professions and occupations...industrial, commercial, creative. An opportunist who knows a good thing when he sees it. Generally...an unobstrusive, benevolent dictator.

Friendship and Love

The affections of the Aquarian are widespread and far-reaching. Cheerful and at ease in any company he makes the best of friends, and his relationships...whether with friend, business-associate or lover...are always good. The air of detachment may be off-putting to those not closely acquainted.

The feeling for suffering at large rather than in the individual extends into the realm of Romantic Love...there exists a preference for universal love rather than personal. Mutual interest is vital for compatibility. Such compatibility leads to lifelong fidelity.

Married life is normally peaceful and tranquil
...more especially if the partner is born under
one of the Signs in Harmony. While not wanting
to boss about the house the innate dislike
of discipline...by others...forbids enforced
obedience. There is a strong love of family...
children instinctively trust the Aquarian...
outside matters and that appearance of aloofness often cause misgiving.

The husband is kind and considerate. Usually
passionate. The wife does not always slide too
gracefully into matrimony but is nevertheless
ably equipped for it. Faithful and loyal herself
she can be astonishingly tolerant in her estima-
tion of those who are not...including the husband. Marriage within the Compatibility or
Harmonious Astrology Sphere can be an
extremely happy marriage indeed!

Summing Up

Positive qualities create a quiet and humane
individual. Of Bohemian tastes but not to an
off-beat degree. Geniality, open-mindedness,
tolerance and straightforwardness predominate.
Malice is seldom borne. Dedication to duty
results in achievement, truth and sincerity and a

brilliant mind all contribute both to material success and spiritual contentment.

The *negative qualities* in the unadvanced Aquarian can be destructiveness, day-dreaming and lack of common sense. By and large the primitive Aquarian can be called inefficient. The breadth of vision bewilders, the wide outlook can be accompanied by deplorable short-sightedness, practical details become lost in a maze of irrelevances. Indecision and procrastination cause a waste of life and the natural aloofness can make him oblivious to the feelings of others. The dislike of imposed discipline is now an intense hatred of all criticism. And the Bohemianism turns nasty, the progressiveness lacks direction and all human relationships suffer in consequence.

Some Famous Aquarians

Kim Novak: Mozart: Lord Byron: Charles Darwin: Abraham Lincoln: Charles Dickens: Colette: Adlai Stevenson: Clark Gable: Eartha Kitt: James Dean.

Aquarians might be described as "reserving their opinion" as far as believers are very convinced that their Sign association is with the

Egyptian Scarab charm...the ancient Khepera... or Keppa...charm. Aquarians are inclined to construct their own Lucky numbers...from beloved telephone numbers, house numbers in streets...even the adding up of the letters in their and others' names. However, as for other Signs, *if* they have any Lucky numbers, they may well be the Positions of the Planets on their Birthdate, zenithally erected.

PISCES (The Fishes)
February 20—March 20

Ruling Planet: Jupiter
Element: Water
Quality: Mutable
Negative
12th House
Gems: Chrysolite, moonstone, ruby and onyx
Colour: Sea green
Metals: Gold and tin
Signs in harmony for companionship, marriage, business: Cancer, Scorpio, Virgo, Libra and Pisces

In General

Like the other Mutables, Pisces dreams much, translates less. The House of Self-Undoing. Mutable Water...and as inconsistent. The two fishes are joined together by a cord...*but are swimming* in opposite directions. The Piscian, kind and gentle, sensitive and melancholy, is also considered unlucky. Possible because of his shy, sensitive, retiring nature which does not permit of the drive and push so often essential in the rat-race of modern times. A dual Personality...consequently an interesting Personality. Bewildering to the subject as well as to others. But this confusion is more than compensated by the Piscian's limitless sympathy and depth of understanding. This duality is revealed in an aggresive attitude in money matters conflicting with a secret love of poverty. It is as though, while aspiring to riches on the face of things, the subconscious interferes to produce unpractical and unrealistic confusion.

There are extremes of mood...elation and despondency. Unless watched, self-pity can cause a great deal of unhappiness. Judgement is emotional rather than intellectually rational. Logic plays a poor second fiddle to *feeling*. This, however, does allow the subject to actually *fee.* deeply and sincerely for others, feeling which is extended to the animal kingdom.

Quiet-natured, he loves quiet. Aspires more than any other to the tranquil life, to rest conten fearlessly and calmly in untroubled solitude.

Health and The Piscian
The stature is usually rather on the small side

and there does not exist the robustness and strength of constitution found in other Signs. Resistance to disease is generally low. The outdoor life is best for the Piscian...with plenty of exercise. The most attractive features are hair ...fine and silky of texture...and the limpid, dreamy eyes. Complexion is, in the majority of cases, fair...with soft skin. There is almost invariably exquisite grace of movement. The smile on the sometimes doleful countenance is like a sudden, brilliant burst of sunshine.

The weakest physical parts of the body are the feet and lungs. Piscians are prone to colds, asthma and bronchial complaints.

Moderation in everything should be the watchword. In middle age the Piscian often puts on weight, becomes quite lethargic. Over-indulgence in all foods and beverages...especially alcohol... should be strictly avoided. Being headstrong and attracted to all kinds of stimulation the hazards resulting from habit-forming sedatives and tranquillizers are not always apparent.

Piscian babies are sometimes extremely delicate and difficult to raise. This is a manifestation of the Piscian mysticism...the Sign being possibly the most mysterious of them all.

Success and The Piscian

What is success? Riches? Finding "Room at the Top"? Contentment? Sublime Romance? Neptune, the Dreamy, conflicts with Jupiter, the Active. But Jupiter is the stronger...instilling the ability to assume shapes and guises.

The ardent desire in Life of the true Piscian is to help others. The subject excels at teaching, nursing, catering, veterinary work, entertaining and welfare. The real sympathy and deep understanding are conductive to all these professions. Yet it is difficult to say that any particular vocation is impossible or unsuitable...except, perhaps, commercial enterprise. Even in this, many, many Piscians, possessing quick tuition, do extraordinarily well. Worldly wealth is seldom the first consideration, so occupations calling for patient, unhurried care for others are obviously most suitable. There is, too, a place for the Piscian in the mystic and occult sciences ...where his psychic gifts can be utilised beneficially for others and, often, remuneratively for himself. He can be a fine spiritual comforter.

Friendship and Love

Friends are easily come by owing to the warmth of heart. There is a tendency to make and worship heroes and, due to the dreamy side of him, he can frequently "play the mug" to the unscrupulous. Acquaintances are also liable to take advantage by sapping energy. Being much of a "backroom boy" he will "pull wires" on behalf of friends exhaustively. People trust the Piscian and want to confide in him, share the burdens of their troubles.

Being extremely sensitive Romance looms large in the Piscian Life. Affection...visibly manifested ...is important. As is the persistent need to be reassured of the loved one's Love. Life without Love is meaningless...Love, that is, in all its aspects.

Married life, provided it is Romantic, appeals strongly. An old world courtesy, a chivalric concern about the loved one's creature comforts ensures smoothness of marital relations despite a prevalent moodiness and an unreliability in matters of provision.

The husband, loving, courteous, affectionate and attentive, will give, and give generously... when he has it. He does not always have it.

The wife is admirably suited to domestic life... with her spirituality, her devotion, her emotional responses and sympathetic understanding. She is the ideal woman to come home to...restful, romantic, house-proud...but not fastidiously so ...and with a wonderful ability to become very much part of the environment.

As parents the Piscians love children around, insist on good education, tend to spoil them, can enter into their world of fantasy.

Summing Up

On the *positive* side there is active sympathy for all beings...human and animal. Given the right circle of friends personal accomplishment may be very high indeed. Sensitivity, lively intelligence and quick tuition, a mind receptive to new and constructive ideas, maintain a well developed, fully integrated Personality able to accept the unchangeable while possessing the knowledge necessary for making such adjustments as Life demands.

Self pity, pessimism and despondency are some of the *negative* qualities of the Sign. Along with persecution mania, a feeling that the world is unsympathetic. The primitive Piscian will withdraw into himself. He will try to escape from reality. He can be his own worst enemy. Yet he possesses no *negative quality* that is not easily adjusted and transformed into a *positive quality* if only he would analyse himself a little, occasionally take a Personal moral inventory by way of a serious study of his Personal Horoscope, where the pitfalls ahead can be watched for and the prognosticated opportunities can be anticipated...and prepared for.

Some Famous Piscians
Elizabeth Taylor: Earl of Snowdon: Chopin: Caruso: Margaret Leighton.

Piscians are great and indefatigable believers in Luck, though they tend to believe it is a quality reserved for others. They sometimes have collections of charms, and the oldest and most persistent are almost certain to be found in their collection...Keppa, the Naga Dragon charm, Talli of Tibet and the ancient Chinese Kiki charm, the latter for the hazards of travel. Lucky numbers are an absolute belief with them. The zenithal presentation of the Positions of the Planets on their Birthdate seems to be the only numbers connected with Piscians...and for any other Sign, for that matter.